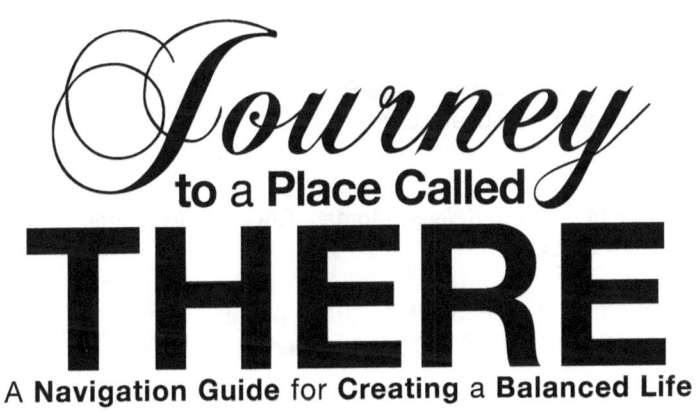

A Navigation Guide for Creating a Balanced Life

Kelly A. Morgan

A Published Work of Scribe, Etc.

www.Scribe-Etc.com / Info@Scribe-Etc.com

Journey to a Place Called THERE is a guide for creating a balanced life. The goal is to help individuals to get "THERE"—which is their ideal place in life—by focusing on the four primary areas of life: Relationships, Health (mental / physical), Spirituality and Finances. For information about special discounts for bulk book purchases, please submit a request to: info@CoachKellySpeaks.com.

Visit our websites: www.Sage-PS.com and www.CoachKellySpeaks.com

Copyright © 2009 Kelly A. Morgan, SAGE Professional Strategies LLC

ISBN-13: 978-0-9823198-0-2 (trade paper)
ISBN-10: 0-9823198-0-0 (trade paper)

All rights reserved. This book in whole or part, may not be reproduced, scanned, photocopied, stored in a retrieval system, transmitted or distributed in any printed or electronic form without prior permission in writing from the publisher.

Published by:

Scribe, Etc.
Stockbridge, Georgia
www.Scribe-Etc.com
info@Scribe-Etc.com

First edition

Printed in the United States of America.

Song lyrics from "Song Of Deliverance," "Just When I Need Him Most" and "Waiting For An Answer," which are featured on the CD "Waiting For An Answer" are reprinted with permission from the songwriter, Minister Darryl F. Cherry.
Copyright © 2009 Dee Cee's Music (All Rights Reserved).

Cover design by KRSmith, www.khrysser.com

This book is dedicated to…

*my mother, Edna H. Kelly Morgan,
who exemplifies the vision of a beautiful,
educated, strong and professional
family-first wife and mother.*

*the loving memory of
my father, William Charles Morgan,
who taught me how to enjoy each day,
appreciate the unconditional love of
family, go after my dreams with
excellence, and disregard the
naysayers who try to
distract me from
any of the above.*

Table of Contents

Author Reflections

Preface

Chapter 1: THERE Is *01*

What Is THERE?
Where Is THERE?
    Personal Reflection Notes

Chapter 2: Where Are You? *09*

When the Unexpected Happens
Work. Life. Balance?
My Journey
    Personal Reflection Notes

Chapter 3: The Compass for Life *21*

Balancing Relationships
    Personal Reflection Questions
Balancing Health
    Minding Your Mind
    Your Physical Health
    Personal Reflection Questions
Balancing Spirituality
    Where Are You Spiritually?

Personal Reflection Questions
Balancing Finances
Budgeting Worksheet
Personal Reflection Questions
Personal Reflection Notes

REST STOP: Enjoy the View 67

Chapter 4: Be the Compass Needle 69

Preparing for the Next Journey
Inspiration: Do As They Did
Personal Reflection Notes

Chapter 5: Destination: THERE 85

Setting Out on Your Destination THERE
Tips for Getting THERE
Inspiration for Your Journey to *Your* Place Called THERE
Personal Reflection Notes

Chapter 6: My Destination THERE Roadmaps 95

Chapter 7: Coach Kelly Speaks 119

The Journey Continues

Other Points of Interest 125

About the Author 137

Author Reflections

There is always someone or several persons who play a major part in the shaping of our lives. For me, there are a number of key individuals who are significant in my life for their own special reasons. Rev. Daddy, the father of a good friend of mine, has said many times to give roses to those deserving of them while they are still living and can enjoy them. So, with that being said, I have a few bouquets of roses to give...

To my mom, Edna H. Kelly Morgan, thank you for being a wonderful role model of a beautiful, educated, strong, professional, family-first wife and mother. Thank you for always being my cheerleader, sounding board and shoulder to lean on. As I get older, I appreciate and recognize more each year the life lessons you and Dad instilled in me to mold me into the lady that I am today. I love you!

To my "little" sister, Tanisha Morgan Coffey, owner of Scribe, Etc., thank you for being the "big sister" when I needed it. I am so proud of you for stepping out into entrepreneurship. Thank you for editing, formatting and publishing this project, my first book. I love you!

To Naomi Smith Oglesby and Dr. Jameelah Gater Richardson, thank you for being more than my best friends since high school, but my sisters for a lifetime. I love you!

To my friend, Deborah Ingram, thank you for sharing your stories of "a place called THERE" moments from your college days and beyond which helped to inspire this book title. I appreciate you including me as family. I love you!

To all of my Morgan-Phillips family, friends, Sorors, Dr. Elliott and Rev. Virginia Cuff, Lincoln Heights Missionary Baptist Church family, Hartford Memorial Baptist Church family and co-workers who prayed with me, prayed for me, provided words of encouragement when the situation looked bleak, celebrated and praised God when my test transformed into my testimony: I sincerely thank you for all of the support! I love you all!

If I have forgotten anyone, please blame this oversight on my mind and not my heart!

My sincerest thanks!

Journey to a Place Called THERE

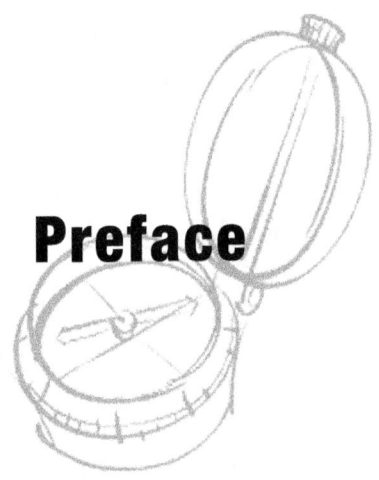

Preface

Thank you for selecting this book. It is your first step towards creating and maintaining a balanced life. It will serve as a guide as you chart your course to the life you desire *and* deserve. As you read, realize that it takes time and deliberate dedication to effectively balance the many ever-changing aspects of your life in order to get to THERE. You cannot do it overnight and your journey will not be without a few bumps in the road because changes in life *are* inevitable and not always controllable. What *can* be controlled is how you manage, react to and work through the change process. This book is designed to help you learn about yourself and the techniques that help you to gain and maintain control. So, congratulations for choosing to take this journey; it will be a memorable trip, to say the least!

In <u>*Journey to a Place Called THERE*</u>, I share my journey. It is a true tale about how it *is* possible to take control of your life and move in a positive and healthy direction, despite how unfairly you think life has treated you.

Through my journey, I realized that there are four primary areas of each of our lives that, when personally prioritized, help to establish and maintain a positive life balance: Relationships, Health, Spirituality and Finances. It is my belief that when you take control of your life, you will find your THERE, a more balanced life!

If you are not living the life you truly desire, you soon will be if you take the advice given in this book. Why? Because it is designed to help you to recognize your current situation and identify some solutions to move towards the life you truly desire for yourself. You do not have to allow yourself to remain powerless and unhappy in your own life. Make the decision today to take back control of your life!

This book was purposely written to be a navigation guide for creating a balanced life; for helping you to create balance in your life. I strongly encourage you to use it to its full capacity. After each section, you will find a *Personal Reflection Notes* page. Like a journal, you can use these note pages to capture key concepts from the book and your personal thoughts as they relate to each section.

Chapter Three, "The Compass for Life," is structured a little differently from the other chapters. In addition to the *Personal Reflection Notes* page, there are *Personal Reflection Questions* after each of the primary life area sections. I encourage everyone, and especially those of you who feel your life is already properly balanced, to answer the *Personal Reflection Questions*. If you are satisfied with how you prioritize and manage the four primary areas of life, Congratulations! What is your plan for maintaining this happy balance? What preparations have you made to weather the storms that are sure to come your way? How can you elevate your situation from good to great?

In Chapter Five you will be getting revved up for your journey and in Chapter Six, you will find the *My Destination THERE Roadmaps for Balancing Relationships, Balancing Health, Balancing Spirituality and Balancing Finances.* This is your opportunity to capture not only your overall thoughts, but to also develop a specific plan for yourself to begin to move you through your personal roadmap to a balanced life.

Best wishes on your
journey to your place called THERE!

Journey to a Place Called THERE

1

THERE Is...

A balanced life is filled with happy times and fond memories as well as unexpected obstacles and frustrating detours. As we navigate through life on the journey to a place called THERE, we must direct our actions and attention towards reaching our ultimate goals in various areas of life, not the obstacles of today. How well we manage these roadblocks in life will make the difference in when and if we reach our destination—THERE.

What Is THERE?

THERE is uniquely defined by each of us. THERE may be a physical location, an emotional state of mind or a realized dream. In some instances it may be a combination of all three. Allow me to introduce you to a few friends in the following scenarios...

Introducing Yvette, the graduate student:

For the Thanksgiving holiday this year, all of Yvette's family has decided to meet at her grandmother's house. This will be the first time in more than 20 years that all of the aunts, uncles and cousins have been together for any occasion. Yvette has not seen some of her cousins in over 10 years. Most family members are aging gracefully, but she does realize that tomorrow is not promised. Therefore, she appreciates every opportunity to create more happy memories with them. All of her family travels from various states throughout the U.S. This impromptu family reunion brings 50 people together for a fun-filled weekend of food, games, picture taking and building bonds within the family. Yvette's excitement of being at her grandmother's house with her family for the holidays <u>leads her to her place called THERE.</u>

Introducing Neil, the entrepreneur:

Six years after opening his first restaurant with minimal funds to invest, Neil's business is flourishing. He is in the process of upgrading his menu as well as remodeling space at a larger, mainstream location. He is hopeful that his new location and menu offerings will entice new customers to patronize his dine-in and catering services. However, as with any construction project and major business venture, various obstacles and time delays have caused Neil significant frustration. For Neil, THERE is completing the journey to this new restaurant opening. Once he opens at the new location, <u>his initial dream will become his reality.</u> Though he is *experiencing some frustrations now, Neil knows that this will make him better prepared for his next journey to a new place called THERE: Franchising!*

Introducing Sebastian and Madison, the honeymooners:

The newlywed couple is on their honeymoon at an all-inclusive resort in the Caribbean. The wedding ceremony was wonderful. The reception was a lot of fun with family and friends all around. Now they are at the resort alone. Of course, other guests are vacationing at the same resort, but the happy couple only has eyes for each other. No matter the weather or who may be physically near them, they are in their own world where nothing matters except being with one another. As this couple enjoys room service breakfasts, romantic candle-lit dinners for two and slow walks along the beach by moonlight, they feel they have arrived. Sebastian and Madison have <u>emotionally elevated to their own private</u> place they call THERE.

As you can probably surmise by now, the look, the feel, the timing, the overall journey to a place called THERE will be different for everyone, because we are all at various stages in life; we all have responsibilities and commitments in various areas of life to balance.

Kelly A. Morgan

Where Is There?

Now, since THERE is a destination that will change throughout life, it is important to learn how to get THERE with the least amount of resistance. So, for experiment's sake, let's level the playing field for a moment and say that we are all on the same journey. Imagine that the following scenario is a detour life has sent you on...

You are married with three children and a dog living in Hometown, USA. You and your spouse have been working steadily in your career fields for 15 years. You own a home and have two more years of payments on the car you bought and a three-year lease on the other car. You have a small college fund set aside for each of the children. With the dual-income, you are able to pay all of the necessary bills each month, but do not have the robust savings account that you would hope to have at this point in your life. Each year, you try to save more money to obtain the minimum of six months of savings the financial planners suggest you have...just in case of an emergency. When you go into work today, you are called to an impromptu department meeting. You arrive to find that the meeting is with your department leadership team and the Human Resources Manager. A business decision has just re-organized you and your co-workers out of a job—effective immediately. You will receive a "generous" severance package of two weeks of pay and medical coverage through the end of the month. What do you do? How will you adjust the various aspects of your life to steady this unexpected imbalance? Write your response on the *Personal Reflection Notes* page.

The reactions to the scenario and responses to the questions above will be different for everyone simply because of the different life experiences that have shaped how you view and handle life. Because of those life experiences, and where you are today, each of you will have a different THERE that you would want to journey to if the above scenario really happened to you. So, are you ready to get personal? I hope so because it is time to focus on you and to determine where you are on your journey to THERE.

Kelly A. Morgan

Personal Reflection:
Notes

_____
_____
_____
_____
_____
_____
_____
_____
_____
_____
_____
_____
_____
_____
_____
_____

www.CoachKellySpeaks.com *or* **www.SAGE-PS.com**

Journey to a Place Called THERE

2

Where Are You?

Life is short. We should all make the most of each and every day. Unfortunately, most of us fail to do so. Instead, we just accept the situations that come into our life rather than make the necessary provisions to have the life we truly desire, because it *seems* easier. However, taking the "easy" way out is what puts us in a rut, a cycle of life occurrences that are unfulfilling and goals that are unrealized. For instance, what sense does it make to profess the same New Year's resolution each year?

How often are you going to start a new diet?

When will you begin to contribute to your 401(k)?

When is it really the "right time" to start a family?

When are you going to finish your college degree?

When are you going to get back in the church?

When are you going to travel the world?

Maybe the better question is:

What is stopping you?

If your intuitive response is "Life," that is your first clue that your life may be out of balance.

When "Life" is what is stopping you from getting to THERE, then perhaps certain aspects of your life are not prioritized the way you would prefer. Instead, certain aspects are prioritized based upon how *you feel they must be* at this particular time. Why is that? At this particular time in your life, what are the controlling factors that are making the "final decision" on how things must be prioritized in your life? How long will you allow these factors to control your life?

Consider this: What would your life look like if you rearranged your priorities? Specifically, in what ways and what areas would your life be different? How would you feel about making these changes in your life?

Please understand, there will always be a need to rearrange various aspects in life. The questions to ask are *when* and *why* certain changes may seem necessary at particular times. When life becomes unbalanced and other forces—in the form of persons or events—take over and reprioritize your life for you, that is a problem. When you have lost control of your life, you need to make the decision to do something about it. You need to take back control of your life.

When the Unexpected Happens

Unexpected actions can be wonderful surprises or devastating nightmares. A phone call. A face-to-face meeting. An airplane crash. A terrorist attack. A successful surgery. The birth of a child. A threat of a hurricane hitting land. A presidential election. An inspirational sermon. A marriage proposal. There are many things that have the ability to change you.

It is really amazing what a difference a day can make in the direction of your life. When the unexpected is positive, you revel in the excitement and enjoy the moment. When the unexpected is negative, how you react and the next steps you take can significantly alter not only the present situation, but also your future.

You can probably imagine how you might manage a major life-changing event. But when one actually creeps up on you and disrupts your life, what do you do? When you look around and no one else is being vocal about this major change, what do you do? Do you continue to sit quietly also? At what expense? How much will your silence cost you? To these questions, everyone's answers will vary. We all have different degrees of acceptance—thresholds of pain, as I like to call it.

Consider Donovan's situation:

> *Donovan is a hard-working, dedicated employee who worked his way up the corporate ladder on the high-potential "watch list" for twenty years. He was doing very well balancing his life between work and family.*

One day, Donovan's employer made it clear that the company was to be the priority; that he needed to be available and ready to work, or report to work, at all times. It was that day that Donovan was finally forced to make a life decision. He had to choose between his family and his high-potential track career.

Donovan decided that he did not want to lose his family as he tried to ride the corporate train up the track. So, Donovan asked to be taken off the high-potential watch list. He still worked and continued to be productive as he watched his peers continue up the corporate track. Donovan worked for another 12 years before retiring with almost 30 years of service...and with his supportive, loving family by his side.

What would you do if you were presented with the same ultimatum as Donovan?

What is your threshold of pain?
How much are you willing to tolerate?
Is your threshold of acceptance based on achieving a certain salary? Title? Office location? Bonus level?

It is important to recognize when you are close to reaching your threshold, so you can prepare yourself for the decisions you will need to make. Perhaps the factors that established the initial "threshold boundaries" are no longer relevant, or not as relevant as expected. Being aware so you can be prepared for how life happens as opposed to letting life happen and negatively affecting you is the key to life balance.

Work. Life. Balance?

Work-Life Balance. Such a simple sounding phrase, but yet often difficult to manage. Most of us have to work to earn money and sustain a certain quality of life. Therefore, working does have a purpose. The question is: How significant is the purpose of work and how does it relate to other aspects of life?

Why is it so easy to get caught up in the roller coaster of work while family and personal life are put on hold, forced to wait for their due time and attention?

What is the magnetic force that draws a person to work 12 to 16 hour days, six to seven days each week? What draws people to answer business calls while on the ski lift on vacation with their family?

Is it the money? Is it job security? Is it the perception of always being abreast of every situation?

How would life be different if you put 100% into work and 100% into your personal life, but with a balance?

There is a time and a place for everything: work, family, friends and self (which includes your health, your spirituality, and your finances). All of these facets of life need to be aligned and balanced. Yes, the weight each area is given will fluctuate over time and situations. That is to be expected. Likewise, each person's list of areas will differ. What still remains to be true is the need to have a comfortable balance to live the life you desire.

Kelly A. Morgan

My Journey

You never think IT could happen to you until IT does. I was thrown into a devastating, real-life nightmare while working as a Human Resources Manager of a large company.

Although I worked in Human Resources for years, I was new to this particular industry and realized that I still had a learning curve in understanding the intricate details of the business. This, of course, would be needed in order to move up in the organization. My desire was to learn all that I could to continue to prepare myself for future promotions. I eventually learned that I needed experience working in different divisions of the company to be well rounded enough to achieve future promotions. To my surprise and excitement, an announcement was posted for two division positions within the company. Although I did not feel I learned all that I could in my current role, these types of division positions were few and far between. I decided I should submit my resume for consideration. After all, I did meet most of the job posting qualifications.

Since my direct supervisor was scheduled to be out of the office during the upcoming week, on Sunday afternoon I sent an e-mail from my personal e-mail address to inform my manager of my desire to apply for both positions. On Monday morning, she agreed and in my mind, all was well. However, on Friday afternoon of that same week, I was called into my manager's office. I was informed that I had been investigated that week. My Internet searches on my computer had been reviewed to see which sites I viewed and how often. I was being accused of using company property for non-work related purposes. After more than ten years in Human Resources, I had never been on this side of the disciplinary process. I felt numb and confused. All I could do was sit in silence and total disbelief.

"What sparked all of this?" you ask.

My signature line on my personal e-mail message referenced "SAGE Professional Strategies, HR Consultant, Business and Leadership Coach." Yes, an email signature changed my life.

Let me give you some background information. A few years **before** interviewing for this position, I started my consulting and leadership coaching business. My business was no secret to the company. Prior to accepting the offer of employment, I disclosed my business. The Senior Human Resources leadership team members were aware that I would be continuing my business while being employed. They agreed. I formally accepted the offer and began working a few weeks later.

Now fast-forward a few years later. A new Human Resources leadership team was now in place. This new leadership team had a problem with my external business venture. They saw my business as a violation of the Ethics Policy for being a potential conflict of interest. I was told that I *must* choose to either maintain my business or my employment. Talk about living a nightmare and experiencing a wide range of emotions!

Despite the angry and trembling feeling I felt inside, I managed to maintain my composure. I did not yell or even speak unprofessionally. I did not cry, but I was firm and specific with my comments. I completely disagreed that there was any type of conflict of interest—potential or actual. I knew I had done nothing wrong. I also knew that there was more behind this investigation of me than was actually being said. My comments and actions in that meeting shaped the upcoming discussions we had over the next month. I attempted to come to a win-win resolution for my employer and me. They held firm to the ultimatum they gave me, but did extend the timeline for my decision.

For obvious reasons, this caused a significant amount of stress, anxiety and depression for me. I was suddenly faced with making life-changing decisions that I never anticipated having to make. My personal plan was to continue to work my way up the corporate ladder while also slowly building my coaching business in my spare time—on weekday nights and the weekends.

In trying to manage this life-changing situation, I suffered from migraine headaches multiple times each week that grew to migraine headaches all day, each day. Since I had no appetite, I stopped eating and lost a lot of weight. I felt like my life was quickly spiraling out of control. I was very concerned about how I could manage taking care of my health and my household expenses. I quickly started looking for another job and went into financial survival mode. I cancelled my 401(k) contribution and cut unnecessary expenses at home—cable movie channels, bi-weekly lawn service, and unlimited long distance on the home phone. I streamlined my errands and frivolous spending. I stopped dining out as much and began cooking at home more. Although I had money saved for the future, I certainly never expected to need to use it at this point in my life.

Determined not to give up on my dream of building a successful coaching business in exchange for a corporate position with no guarantee for the future, I found myself at a crossroad in my life. I quickly realized that this situation was much larger than me and that there was no way I would be able to successfully maneuver my way through on my own. I immediately turned to God in prayer. I asked for peace of mind, direction and clarity on what I needed to do.

Before moving forward, I tried to reflect back to understand how this imbalance in my life could have occurred. I could not fathom that I was the only hard-working corporate employee whose life seemed to revolve around work. Admittedly, allowing work to become the center of my life was not planned. It just seemed to happen that way over time. Given the environment of my department and the overall culture of the company, I did not see the possibility of a drastic change in the role work played in my life in the near future; not working for that company or any other if I was able to move to a lateral position. At that point, I knew that I was at a crossroad; not just in my corporate career, but in my life overall. Life as I knew it was officially over. Quickly, the comfort and security I felt from having a consistent job and paycheck for more than a decade faded away. I felt like my world went dark. At times, even in the sunniest daylight hours, the world looked a dark gray in my subconscious mind. I felt like I was free-falling and falling and falling still. Other times, I felt like I was being pulled down in quick sand. Needless to say, it was a challenge pulling myself out of the darkness and depression that I felt. Those around me tried to help. The reality was, it was my life, my decisions that had led me to where I was and I was the only person who could get myself to THERE, where I really wanted to be.

I knew I had to first acknowledge the problem and to be honest with myself. Mentally I had to take several steps back and look at the situation as a whole. Being forced to live this nightmare reminded me of the importance of having a balance in life. That was something that I realized I was lacking. It became even clearer to me that relationships, health, and spirituality are my primary life areas that have to be in sync and balanced in order for me to live a happy life. Having control over finances in life is equally important because the strength and weakness of finances certainly affect each of the primary life areas.

Stay tuned for the rest of my journey. In the meantime, let's take a closer look and explore each primary life area.

Journey to a Place Called THERE

Personal Reflection:
Notes

Kelly A. Morgan

3

The Compass for Life

As with any trip, regardless of the distance to travel, at a minimum you must know your ultimate destination. A roadmap and a compass are the tools you will need for a successful journey. The roadmap will show you where you currently are located and illustrates your surroundings. It will also allow you to review, prepare and highlight your preferred route on paper. Meanwhile, the compass will help keep you focused and on course to ensure your ultimate arrival to your destination. As you move through your journey, the needle on the compass adjusts to show your actual position at any given time: north, south, east or west. Obstacles such as the weather, construction and reliability of your transportation may cause delays in the journey, but they do not have to put an end to the trip overall.

Consider this: The trip, the overall journey, represents Life. The navigation guide, the roadmap showing the path to take to reach your destination, is this book. The needle on the Compass for Life adjusts towards the four directions, the four primary areas of life: Relationships, Health, Spirituality and Finances.

As you travel through life, you will need to continuously adjust your position to create the appropriate balance. Again with life being full of daily changes, it will be necessary to make adjustments in the four primary areas of life as you remain focused on reaching your ultimate destination—a place called THERE.

Let's discuss each primary area of life and how it directly affects the overall life journey and life balance.

Balancing Relationships

Life gets so busy at times that we forget to take time to demonstrate love and fellowship with others. Friends and family are important and should never be taken for granted. Having time with your spouse, significant other, children, family and friends is priceless and not promised. Taking family trips and just spending time together at home builds the bond of closeness and creates lasting memories.

I remember going to the drive-in movies with my parents. My sister and I put on our pajamas, got our pillows and Mom brought popcorn for us to snack on. What's a drive-in movie without popcorn? On some weekends, our family played board games, card games and watched movies. Our family also loved watching basketball! I remember the 1989 NBA Playoffs vividly. The Detroit

Journey to a Place Called THERE

Pistons swept the LA Lakers with a playoff record of 4-0 in the NBA Finals that year. I can still see my Dad now. During the last minutes of the game, he ran to the closet and grabbed a broom. Then we all—Mom, Dad, my sister, and I—began chanting as he "swept" the carpet in the family room. We all shouted, "Sweep, sweep, sweep L-A! Sweep, sweep, sweep L-A!" in sync with the fans on TV. The Pistons took home the first title in team history that night and we were so animated and excited that the next morning Dad and I were hoarse! I remember it like it was yesterday. When is the last time you created memories with your family and friends? Taking time off from work and scheduling quick weekend trips or even short evening visits are options to keeping the closeness of family and friends alive. It is very easy to get caught up in the fast pace of life, and to forget to reevaluate what is really important.

Two of my best girlfriends and I like to do teleconferences. We get on a three-way phone call for two hours at a time every couple of months. Of course, we talk to each other individually between the teleconferences. But when the three of us are on the call we can get everyone's updates, give advice, make fun of each other and plan our next girls' weekend. Since we live in three different states, this is how we make sure to stay in touch.

When times start to get rough, your friends and family are the ones who can help. They are also the ones who can very gently, or with tough love, let you know when and how your life is unbalanced. They may not be able to fix the problem, but as someone who is close to you who has a view from the outside looking in, they can help to support you. You, of course, can do the same for them when the time comes. And, it will.

As a parent, aunt or uncle, daughter or son, spouse, grandchild, cousin or very dear friend, having quality family time is important for nurturing your relationships. Watching the high school gymnastics meets, chaperoning school trips, escorting your daughter to the Daddy-Daughter Dance, visiting out-of-town family, golfing with your son, having dinner together and just being together with no specific agenda. Those are some of the important quality times that memories are made of and last a lifetime. Of course, having a stable income and available finances provide the means for the family trip, golf games, and the place you call home. We will talk more on balancing finances later.

Looking from the other end of the spectrum, every person and relationship is not supposed to last for years and years. I believe people are in our lives for a season and for a reason. Everyone is not destined to continue the journey of life with you. Some may be too negative and will hold you back from your intended greatness. You can love a person from a distance when it may be too toxic to love them in your close personal space. Everyone does not deserve a front row seat in your life. You may not wish any ill-will on them, but you do not truly need them in your life. This may sound mean and rather arrogant. But, if you are honest with yourself, you will soon realize who is truly a helpful addition to your life and who causes you more heartache and pain by trying to continue the relationship. This person may be a family member, childhood friend, neighbor, or co-worker.

Journey to a Place Called **THERE**

Have you heard the saying: When someone shows you their true colors, believe them? Maybe you are completely surprised and think their behavior is so unlike them. Think about this: How likely is it that their current behavior is actually their true personality? Perhaps this is just the first display of their true personality that you have recognized? Think back to other small situations and comments that may have rubbed you the wrong way, but you overlooked it as being nothing. Is it still really nothing or starting to add up to something that you should not have to tolerate in your life? If someone tells you they are not good for you, trust the internal soul-searching they must have done to come to the realization. Then, appreciate the fact that they respect you enough to not continue to be a negative influence or anchor in your life. Thank them for their honesty and unselfishness. Take heed to their message and remove them from your life. Understand they may never be a part of your life again. Hold on to the positive memories, learn from the life lessons and look forward to your future ahead!

It's all about you! You want to surround yourself with people and environments that are positive additions to your life. Realistically, this can be a challenge. If you are growing in your life and establishing the foundation for greatness and achieving success, but others around you are not growing at all or perhaps at the same rate, there could be tension. Others may not understand why you feel the need to distance yourself from "friends." This is when you must dig deep within and be true to yourself.

Through college I had a group of friends that I socialized with most often. Some of us went to different colleges, but still stayed in touch and continued the friendship after college as well. We all earned degrees in various disciplines. Some of us pursued graduate degrees right away, while others began in our professional careers. As we grew into adulthood, the price tag on our fun excursions grew as well. Being young, single, full-of-life professionals, most of us managed our financial responsibilities well enough to accommodate our trips and excursions. There was one friend who often made comments about not having the money like we did for various reasons. I assumed this person was feeling a bit self-conscious since they were not at the professional or financial place in life as they expected to be at that time. We never treated this person any differently though. After all, we were all friends!

Now fast-forward in your mind. Some friends were getting married. Some were starting families. Some of us were relocating to other states. Some were building homes. Some were testing the waters of entrepreneurship. All of us were at different points in life, but no matter how busy life became, we still found time to have fun! Fast forward a few more years. We all decided to go on a weekend ski trip. After months of planning, cabin arrangements confirmed, and final deposits made, one person decided to back out of the trip at the last minute for financial reasons. Yes, the same friend. Once again, the group was forced to absorb the extra cost since this person did not contribute their expenses as they promised and committed to do. Over the years this pattern of selfishness and mismanagement of funds weighed heavily on the friendship.

Long story short, we realized that ultimately this person did not have the same values and was finally showing their true self. Perhaps, we were just then recognizing what was actually showing all along. It was from that point forward that I decided to distance myself from that "friend."

Part of having life balance is distancing yourself from friends, acquaintances and any others that are negative influences or negative energy in your life. Are you going out of your way and disrupting the flow and advancements in your life to help support and bail out loved ones? Are you trying harder to help them over and over again more than they are actually helping themselves? Step back. Ask yourself, "Is this what is best for me? What am I losing or gaining? Is this a healthy relationship?"

The question of healthy versus unhealthy relationships is not specific only to individuals. It also applies to any major commitments that affect your personal life. For most people the biggest non-human relationship commitment is work. So, I have to ask: Are you working so much that you no longer have any time to spend with your family or enjoy other outings with those you care about? My guess is that on some level you are. And for what? To maintain material possessions? Is it *really* worth it?

When evaluating the relationships in your life, consider both what the relationship is allowing you to do and what obstacles it may be placing in your way. Family and *true* friends are priceless jewels in our lives and should be treated as such. Tomorrow is not promised, so make the most of today.

Kelly A. Morgan

Personal Reflection:
Relationships

Describe your level of satisfaction with the relationships you have with your family and friends.

<u>What</u> are you tolerating?

_____
_____
_____
_____
_____
_____
_____

<u>Who</u> are you tolerating?

_____
_____
_____
_____
_____
_____
_____

Journey to a Place Called THERE

What is working well with balancing your relationships?

_____
_____
_____
_____
_____
_____
_____
_____

Key messages for you from the Balancing Relationships section...

_____
_____
_____
_____
_____
_____
_____

Kelly A. Morgan

Balancing Health

Live. Laugh. Love.

~ Unknown Author

Life is not measured by the number of breaths we take, but by the number of moments that take our breath away.

– Unknown Author

Are these just nice sayings that we hang on our walls at home and put on our desk at work, or, are they your mantras for life?

Everybody is different. Your mental stability, the amount of rest you allow yourself, physical activities and your diet all play a part in your overall health. Therefore, you must work to keep your physical and mental health in optimal condition.

Minding Your Mind

Since your state of mind affects your happiness each day and how you interact with others, your overall mental health and stability are very important. You should always be cognizant of what you are feeding your mind. For example, each of us wants to live a rich, happy and successful life. But here is the million dollar question:

"How do *you* define richness, happiness, and success?"

In this materialistic world, a person's wealth may be defined by the size of their house, the number of cars they own, or how much money they have to spend on luxury items. Happiness may be defined by how large the entourage is of a person who likes being seen with a crowd. Success may be in comparing a person to other well-known success stories. However, being successful generally means how well you are "keeping up with The Joneses". Well, who said what The Joneses have is also good for you? Do you really know what happens in The Joneses home when all of the new friends have gone away and they are in the empty home alone?

Define the richness of your own life.

Sometimes trying to imitate another person's life can be more detrimental to your own health. You may make decisions for your life and family that leave you so stressed that they cause diseases to flare up and illness to fall upon you that may have been avoidable or controllable.

Taking care of your mental health also means paying attention to the thoughts you allow to enter and stay in your mind. For example, if we hold on to nasty comments people have made in the past, their premonitions of a bleak future, or our broken hearts and our shattered dreams, where will that take us in life? Nowhere! At some point, we must pull ourselves up and recognize that words may sting initially, but scars do fade away in time. Be strong to prove, not to the naysayers of your past, but to yourself, that you have a significant purpose in this life. Your future can be as great as the dreams you can visualize for yourself.

Mental health is tricky. Sometimes, what is plaguing your mind can reveal itself physically. That is why it is important to pay attention to what your body is telling you. I did. I worked in a fast-paced corporate Human Resources department. I realized that I suffered from migraine headaches several times each week. Initially, the migraines were after work. They expanded to affecting me during most of the workday each day. It is not normal or healthy to have such extreme headaches so frequently. My body was screaming at me to pay attention and make some drastic changes before changes were made for me. I decided it was time to redesign my life. With a lot of prayer, I started to follow my heart and do what felt right for my life overall. Within several weeks of making that decision and making drastic changes in life, the migraines came less fierce and less frequently.

The pain I felt from the migraine headaches was how my mind let me know my mental health was out of balance. I desperately needed to make more time to rest my mind, and the excruciating migraines certainly forced me to do just that.

Do not wait to feel the pain of migraine headaches to take control of your mental health. Here are a few tips to allow enough time each day for rest and relaxation of your mind:

Journey to a Place Called THERE

- Plan your days so you can get enough restful sleep each night so that your mind and body can rejuvenate and be energized for the next day.

- Schedule time to pamper yourself for basic hygiene and well-being. Take a bubble bath or book a full-body massage. This quiet time allows your mind to wind down and take a break from all of the thoughts that run through it every moment of every day.

- Take 20-30 minutes each morning to prepare for the upcoming day. You may choose to use this time to meditate, pray, read a book or write in your personal journal. When you allow for alone time with yourself, it allows your mind to ease into your day and to begin the positive thoughts and energy you can carry with you throughout your day!

- You may choose to simply sit outside and enjoy the fresh air! If instead, you want to relax in the company of others, you may choose to watch a movie or your favorite TV show with friends, play with the family dog, or make a call to talk to some friends, family and loved ones that you have not spoken with recently.

The ultimate purpose is to do what feels best for you so that you can relax your mind to strengthen your overall mental health. You may prefer to spend some time alone or to be in the presence of others. Whatever you choose is right because it is right for you.

Your Physical Health

Sometimes we are able to successfully change our eating habits and exercise routine as a method for improving our physical health.

Unfortunately, with our fast-paced lives, we do not always take the time needed to attend to our bodies. For instance, how often do you opt for a not-so-healthy but ever-so-convenient fast food drive-thru meal over making a healthy meal at home? Or worse, how many times have you sworn that for your New Year's resolution you were going to join a gym and start a serious workout plan? Do not beat yourself up if I have described you to a tee. You are not alone and it is hard when beginning a healthier lifestyle because it does take so much commitment, time and money. But, once you realize that you are worth all of the effort, because you will never get THERE if you are not healthy enough for the journey, living healthily becomes easier. The transition starts with adopting one main habit: Pay attention to what you are putting into your body. To do so you can:

- Eat more baked, broiled and grilled foods and limit the amount of fried foods in your diet.

- Consciously take the time to eat slower, which allows you to not only savor your meal more but also for your body to tell you when you are full.

- Eat more frequently during each day and be sure to eat before you are overly hungry; chances are better that you will make wiser food choices and eat smaller portions.

- Cut back on chemically processed foods and replace them with fresh fruits and vegetables. Shopping at a farmer's market where everything is fresh is a good idea, and fresh fruits and fresh vegetables are typically less expensive.

- Take vitamins that are appropriate for your body's needs. I suggest that you discuss this with your physician first.

You have to pay attention to your body and what it is telling you—mentally and physically. You must have regular physical examinations to catch any signs of changes sooner. Early detection can be the key to successful treatment and recovery. It is also important to incorporate exercise into your everyday lifestyle. Here are a few tips to get you started:

- Walk the treadmill or elliptical while watching TV or listening to music on your iPod. If you do not have access to gym equipment, walk around the track at the local high school or around the halls of a shopping mall.

- Meet up with friends at the neighborhood gym to participate in aerobics, yoga, spinning and other classes offered.

- Whenever possible, take the stairs instead of the escalator or elevator.

- Park at the end of the row when you go grocery shopping, to the mall, or wherever. Your body will appreciate the extra steps you are taking—literally and figuratively—to improve your physical health.

Since people are at different places in their eating habits, exercise regime and overall health, how one manages his or her health will be a personal decision. However, do make a decision for the betterment of your physical health! Choosing to make one or two small adjustments can make a long-term improvement in your life. Exercising and being active helps to alleviate stress and keeps your body in shape. Living a healthy life does not have to be difficult. However, it does require your dedication.

Take time...

Time for reflection
And renewal...
Time for beginnings
And growth...
Time for nurturing
And discovery...
Time for you

~ Marjolein Bastin

Journey to a Place Called THERE

Personal Reflection:
Health

Describe your level of satisfaction with the current state of your health.

Describe how you are currently managing your health.

_____
_____
_____
_____
_____
_____
_____
_____

What is working well with balancing your overall health?

_____
_____
_____
_____
_____
_____
_____

What improvements in your health would you like to see?

_____
_____
_____
_____
_____
_____
_____
_____

Key messages for you from the Balancing Health section…

_____
_____
_____
_____
_____
_____
_____

Balancing Spirituality

Be still to listen. Often times we are so busy, that we do not take time to recharge our minds and our bodies. No matter what your spiritual or religious beliefs may be, your faith is where your soul is centered and finds direction for life. Whether you attend church services or mass, meditate and chant, or read and study on your own, allotting time to observe your beliefs and worship in your way is an important element of a balanced life.

You may consider yourself to be a spiritual person who has beliefs of a higher force of nature which helps to control the destiny of your life. You may believe that everything happens for a reason which is based on the decisions that you make for yourself. No matter how you may define your spirituality, you have a part of your life that is centered on explaining how things happen in your life.

I received an inspirational e-mail from a friend with a simple tag line at the end that said, "Remember your situation is not your destination—just preparation!" This short message was a very powerful reminder that we are often times put into situations to learn a lesson and to prepare us for the next journey in life.

This chapter speaks about balancing the spiritual aspect of your life. However you define spirituality and your belief is how you can relate this chapter to your life and your current situation.

Kelly A. Morgan

Where Are You Spiritually?

As we live each day and embark on our journeys through life, we all have our own definitions of spirituality, religion and the presence, or lack of, a supreme being who is over our lives. To paraphrase the Random House Dictionary definitions from the Internet…

> *Spirituality* can be defined as sacred matters or religion; intangible aspects of man such as the mind or soul.
>
> *Religion* can be defined as a specific fundamental set of beliefs and practices agreed upon by a number of persons or sects; something one believs in and follows devotedly; and a strong belief in supernatural powers that control human destiny.
>
> *Supreme Being* or *Deity* can be defined as any super natural being worshipped as controlling some part of the world or some aspect of life who is the personification of a force; the supernatural being conceived as the perfect and omnipotent and omniscient originator and ruler of the universe.

How do you define your spiritual life?

It is important to know how your beliefs and the daily or weekly activities associated with such play a role in the other aspects of your life. Once you have comfortably defined the importance of the spiritual aspect of your life, you will then need to decide if how you are currently living is aligned with your spiritual needs. If not, what changes do you need to make to bring more balance in your life? The Reflection Questions at the end of this section will help you to organize your thoughts.

My Spiritual View

I am a Christian. I grew up in the Baptist Church and have a deep belief in God and His son Jesus Christ. Through my faith, I find my strength and a source of direction for my life. Chapter Three of Proverbs in the Bible says, "Trust in the Lord with all your heart and lean not on your own understanding; in all your ways acknowledge Him, and He will make your paths straight." I sincerely believe the message in this scripture. I believe in turning my problems over to Jesus and letting Him fight my battle. I believe that God does not put more on us than we can bare, but He does test us. I believe the devil is always busy and tempts us to veer away from walking in the path that God has ordained for us. All-in-all, I know God is in control. I know that sometimes what the devil means for evil in our lives, God can transform it and instead use it for good.

Living a life of faith also helps to provide direction for the future. My Pastor, Dr. Elliott Cuff, explains living faithfully as moving ahead without seeing ahead. Living a spiritual life means continuing to be obedient in following the plan God set for your life. Looking for God's grace and favor as opposed to looking for approval from mankind.

Unlike man, God is able to move people in and out of our lives, close and open doors of opportunity, protect us from harm and move us to our next blessing. I believe God puts us in situations and people in our lives to help us in current predicaments while also preparing us for the next blessing. At the same time that I was dealing with the situation at my job that I described earlier, I was also preparing for a choir concert and live CD recording for my church. That hectic rehearsal schedule and the music itself truly helped to keep my sanity and give me peace of mind.

I had not sung in a choir concert since my high school years. It was divine timing that the rehearsals for the CD "Waiting For An Answer" by the Minister of Music, Darryl F. Cherry and performed by my church's mass choir, would be so appropriate for helping me to survive that stressful time in my life. The songs were constantly playing in my mind—either as I sung them by myself, chimed in with the chorus at rehearsal, or listened to the rehearsal CDs; the lyrics rang so true. In preparing for the concert, I listened to CDs of the rehearsals. I would wake up with songs lyrics playing in my head and I went through each day singing them as well. The lyrics are:

> *I tried so hard to change it on my own. I need your help. Forgive me Lord. I want to be used by you. Create in me a clean heart and renew a right spirit in me. I want to go higher in you. Separate me from all my sins. Wash me. Make me. Mold me. Shape me. Appoint me. Anoint me. Choose me. Use me. Forgive me Lord. I want to be used by you.*

He is there.
Always on time to give me peace of mind.
Just when I need Him most.

Waiting for an answer when you've prayed
God has not forgotten you.
He knows just what to do.
Yes! He will answer.
When you've prayed, and you prayed and you
prayed all night long!
Waiting for an answer.
He will answer you.

In addition to singing in the choir and hearing sermons each Sunday from Dr. Cuff, which seemed to speak directly to me, I read inspirational stories and quotes each day. Please see the "Other Points of Interest" chapter for some of the scriptures, poems and quotes that I find helpful to me in various stages of my journey to THERE.

Are You Spiritually Active?

Part of your spiritual responsibility is in moving past yourself to assist others. Giving of your time and talents by working in church ministries, mission trips and other community service projects and organizations can be personally fulfilling while also helping those in the community.

Whatever your faith, whatever and whomever you find your spiritual source of strength, making time to commit yourself to the work you want to do is important. Perhaps your gift is singing in the choir and ministering to the congregation. Perhaps you are a part of the media ministry and monitor the video cameras, microphones, or lights during worship services, weddings and afternoon programs. Perhaps you work well with children and become a part of the Education Department. Whatever your talents, whatever your calling for ministry work and spiritual growth, allowing the time in your weekly schedule to fulfill this desire and responsibility can help other aspects of life to also fall into place.

In the end, when it comes to my spirituality, I do not pretend that my movements through life are orchestrated by me. I strongly believe in divine intervention and that I will reap the blessings and favor of God by being obedient to His word. This is what has worked for me. I also believe that having strong family ties and true friendship bonds can help you through any situation.

This is what works for me from a spiritual perspective. Do you know what works for you?

Journey to a Place Called THERE

Personal Reflection:
Spirituality

Think about your spiritual life and answer the questions below based on your level of satisfaction with it.

Describe your level of satisfaction with your spiritual life.

_____
_____
_____
_____
_____
_____
_____

In what areas would you like to see more spiritual growth?

_____
_____
_____
_____
_____
_____
_____

What is stopping you from having a spiritual life or from having the stronger spiritual connection that you desire?

_____

_____

_____

_____

_____

_____

_____

_____

Key messages for you from the Balancing Spirituality section…

_____

_____

_____

_____

_____

_____

_____

Journey to a Place Called THERE

Balancing Finances

It has been said that love makes the world go around. I believe that is true. However, I also think that having a money tree to pick from would make going around the world more fun! Well, since many of us do not actually have a money tree to pick from, we have to find other means of managing and balancing our finances.

Like a rose with thorns on its stem, you want your finances to be protected. Like the skilled gardener who knows how to handle the rose without destroying the beautiful blossom, you need a financial planner. At least an overall financial plan for how to grow your money and investments year-over-year like a perennial rose bush. A financial planner can *advise* on your overall savings, investments and spending habits, but you are the one who will ultimately make the difference in your life.

Since finances flow through all aspects of life, it is of the utmost importance to have proper understanding, planning and management of them. Do you know how much money comes into and leaves your household each month? Each quarter? Each year? What goals have you set for building and maintaining the lifestyle you desire? What goals and plans do you have for your future?

For the most accurate view of your overall financial picture, you will want to organize your spending and household expenses. There are three main points to consider when organizing your household spending:

1. <u>Fixed Expenses</u>: These are household expenses that you must pay each week, month or quarter, but the amount of each expense is out of your control:
   - home mortgage or apartment rent
   - homeowner's or renter's insurance
   - car note and gasoline
   - home or apartment utilities
   - school costs for your children

2. <u>Controllable</u>: These are household expenses that you may have each week, month or quarter, but the amount of each expense *IS* within your control. Actually, the decision to have some of these expenses are within your control as well:
   - groceries
   - cable television and Internet services
   - dry cleaning
   - lawn service
   - cellular and home phone service
   - extracurricular activities for your children
   - tithes and offering

3. <u>Extras</u>: These are household expenses that you may have each week, month or quarter. The important difference is none of these are necessities of life. They are the "nice to haves" when you have additional money to spend so the decision to incur theses expenses are completely within your control:
   - Purchasing dine-in, carry out, delivery or fast food
   - Shopping for pleasure
   - Personal entertainment (movies, concerts,

plays, travel and vacations)
- Professional, community and social organizational memberships and training

Let's take a look at four points to build the foundation for a life of balanced finances.

1. Calculate your actual net income
   - It is important to understand the total amount of money that is available to spend. It is equally important that you know and calculate how much money is coming into the household each month after taxes and deductions.
   - If payroll deductions are automatically taken before the balance is deposited, include the amount of your income before the deductions.
   - Highlight this number for future reference.

2. Identify your household goals
   - Determine how much money you want to save and in what areas on a monthly and annual basis.
   - Determine how you want to spend your money on a monthly and annual basis. Highlight this number. For example, do you have a goal of:
     o Paying off your 30-year fixed mortgage in 15 years
     o Adding a certain amount of money to your portfolio and 401(k) for investments
     o Being in a position to take a family

vacation each year
- o Being able to pay some of your parent's expenses for them
- o Giving tithes and offering at church or annual donations to a charity

3. Create a detailed list of your current monthly spending
    - List **exactly** where you spend your money each month for household expenses as well as fun/social spending. For quarterly and bi-annual expenses, such as car insurance, include those amounts in monthly increments.
    - List 401(k), health savings accounts (HSA) and other monthly investments you make.

4. Create a detailed household budget of monthly expenses
    - Now that you have identified how much money you bring into the household each month, your overall household goals and current expenses, you can create a monthly budget for future saving as well as spending.
    - Use the *Budgeting Worksheet* at the end of this chapter to track your:
        - o Annual budget per expense
        - o Monthly budget per expense
        - o Actual spending expense per month
        - o Total spent per expense for the year
        - o Total spent per month

Journey to a Place Called THERE

Not everyone likes to deal with numbers, but if you have a goal, reaching your financial THERE can be fun and extraordinarily rewarding. Here are a few tips for meeting financial goals with improved spending and savings:

1. Review your current fixed and controllable house hold expenses to identify any areas where improvements can be made. Some of the fixed costs may be negotiated to lesser expenses with a little bit of research from you. Yes, you should have renter's or homeowner's insurance, but, have you researched various companies to be certain you have the best coverage and price that is available to you? Many of us feel we cannot live without our cell phones, but, is your current plan the best one for your situation?

2. Review your current extra expenses to identify any areas where improvements can be made. These are the "nice to do, but not required each month" items. Everyone wants to have fun and splurge on themselves and their family from time to time. The key is to splurge responsibly and in moderation. Understand how the "extras" will affect the rest of your budget and determine if it is worth it. If so, enjoy! If not, congratulations! You just saved yourself some money (literally) and prevented frivolous spending that could negatively impact the overall household goals you set for yourself.

3. Use one credit card so you will always know your true debt balance. If you have four credit cards and carry a balance of $1500, $2500, $3200 and

$2800 respectively, each card individually may not seem so bad to manage. Maybe you feel you could pay off the $1500 card in one month or the $3200 card over a few months. Remember, when you carry a balance, you pay fees and/or interest each month. If it will take a few months to pay off $3200, how long will it take to pay $10,000—the total you owe for all of the credit cards? Does paying off $10,000 seem as manageable?

4. Use credit cards wisely to build your credit history by paying bills on time. Maximize the rewards on credit cards by taking advantage of the monetary awards, store gift cards and/or frequent flyer miles earned by spending. Perhaps you can use the money awarded from the credit cards and airline frequent flyer miles for upcoming trips. This can directly affect the bottom line of your savings account without extra thought or action from you.

5. Use online banking to pay bills and to track the activity in your credit and savings accounts. Know your credit card and banking interest rates. Saving accounts generally provide higher monthly interest rates than checking accounts. Additionally, when you receive your bill statement, you can immediately log onto your online banking account to schedule your bill payment. This will insure the bill payment will be paid by the scheduled due date. You will also be able to see what financial obligations are coming for each month and to keep track of checks written that have already been processed.

Journey to a Place Called **THERE**

6. Plan your errands to save gasoline and travel less unnecessarily. Also, if you fill up your gas tank between 1/2 and 1/4 full, this will reduce the risk of running out of gas and give you the option of bargain hunting for the best gas prices instead of having to buy from a station just because you are driving on fumes.

7. Be savvy about grocery shopping and restaurant dining. Prepare meals at home based on sale items at the grocery store and stock up whenever possible. You can prepare your lunch, which reduces the cost of eating out for the lunch. Subscribe to restaurant newsletters and e-mail lists to get coupons and dining specials. Some restaurants offer "kids eat free" nights and "buy one-get-one dinner for two" promotions, which can maximize your spending while also providing a night out for the family.

8. Organize and de-clutter your home. You will be surprised at how many extra toothbrushes, bottles of deodorant, shower soap, dish detergent, rolls of toilet paper and bottles of nail polish remover you may already have in your home. If your shelves (and your life) are cluttered, you will not be able to see what you have and will waste money buying more and more unnecessarily.

9. Family entertainment can be fun, but does not have to be expensive. Join movie clubs that allow you to view as many movies as you so desire each month for one base price. The movies come

directly to your mailbox. Or, borrow books and movies from the library. Play board games as a family. Go to the park. Check out the local paper for free events around town, too.

10. Make a shopping list for any kind of shopping you do; whether you are going to the mall or the grocery store—make a list! A list will help to keep you on track for the reason you are shopping and should curve impulse purchases.

11. If possible, live on one income in a dual-income household. To stretch your paycheck even further, pay yourself when you get an increase in your hourly rate or base salary. Simply because you make more does not mean you must spend more.

12. Use cash. Go to the bank once a week or bi-weekly and take out the cash you have budgeted for your groceries, fun, gas, and other expenses that are not bills. Then, pay for those things with cash. The idea behind this is that you will be more conscious of the money you are spending if you can steadily see it dwindling every time you take your wallet out.

The underlying theme is to be aware of how and where you are spending your hard-earned income. As author Fredrick Wilcox said, "Progress involves risk. You can't steal second base and keep your foot on first." By setting goals and working towards them, you will be pleasantly surprised at how more aligned other aspects of life can be as you work your financial plan and invest more in yourself.

I encourage you to use the budgeting worksheet each month to keep you on your financial plan. To download the full version of the *Budget Worksheet*, visit my Web site at www.CoachKellySpeaks.com

Taking the time to pay attention to what is happening in your life today will prepare you for what is to come tomorrow. Please do not feel that you must master how to successfully balance each of these primary areas of life. No one is perfect. Besides, life presents new challenges to each of us each day. However, the tips in this book will help you to make better choices! You will see the difference by learning how to acknowledge your place in life, recognizing when and how life changes, and how the changes affect your overall journey to your destination. While you are on your journey to a place called THERE, you will learn to be the compass needle for your life. You will learn how to adjust the priorities in your life, in the primary areas, to maintain your overall life balance.

There is no time like the present. So, how about getting started on tracking your finances right now? The following *Budgeting Worksheet* will surely help!

Kelly A. Morgan

Budgeting Worksheet

Household Expenses	Annual Budget	Monthly Budget
Mortgage / Rent		
Utilities		
Car Note		
Car Gasoline		
Home Phone		
Cellular Phone		
Cable TV		
Internet		
Groceries		
Insurance:		
- Health		
- Car		
- Home / Renter's		
Travel & Fun		
Clothing		
Daycare		
Other:		
Other:		
Other:		
TOTAL		

www.CoachKellySpeaks.com *or* www.SAGE-PS.com

Actual Expenses - 1st Qtr.

Household Expenses	Jan.	Feb.	Mar.	Total
Mortgage / Rent				
Utilities				
Car Note				
Car Gasoline				
Home Phone				
Cellular Phone				
Cable TV				
Internet				
Groceries				
Insurance:				
- Health				
- Car				
- Home / Renter's				
Travel & Fun				
Clothing				
Daycare				
Other:				
Other:				
Other:				
TOTAL				

Kelly A. Morgan

Actual Expenses - 2nd Qtr.

Household Expenses	Apr.	May	Jun.	Total
Mortgage / Rent				
Utilities				
Car Note				
Car Gasoline				
Home Phone				
Cellular Phone				
Cable TV				
Internet				
Groceries				
Insurance:				
- Health				
- Car				
- Home / Renter's				
Travel & Fun				
Clothing				
Daycare				
Other:				
Other:				
Other:				
TOTAL				

www.CoachKellySpeaks.com *or* www.SAGE-PS.com

Actual Expenses - 3rd Qtr.

Household Expenses	Jul.	Aug.	Sep.	Total
Mortgage / Rent				
Utilities				
Car Note				
Car Gasoline				
Home Phone				
Cellular Phone				
Cable TV				
Internet				
Groceries				
Insurance:				
- Health				
- Car				
- Home / Renter's				
Travel & Fun				
Clothing				
Daycare				
Other:				
Other:				
Other:				
TOTAL				

Kelly A. Morgan

Actual Expenses - 4th Qtr.

Household Expenses	Oct.	Nov.	Dec.	Total
Mortgage / Rent				
Utilities				
Car Note				
Car Gasoline				
Home Phone				
Cellular Phone				
Cable TV				
Internet				
Groceries				
Insurance:				
- Health				
- Car				
- Home / Renter's				
Travel & Fun				
Clothing				
Daycare				
Other:				
Other:				
Other:				
TOTAL				

www.CoachKellySpeaks.com *or* www.SAGE-PS.com

Journey to a Place Called THERE

Total Comparisons

Household Expenses	Annual Budget	Annual Expenses
Mortgage / Rent		
Utilities		
Car Note		
Car Gasoline		
Home Phone		
Cellular Phone		
Cable TV		
Internet		
Groceries		
Insurance:		
- Health		
- Car		
- Home / Renter's		
Travel & Fun		
Clothing		
Daycare		
Other:		
Other:		
Other:		
TOTAL		

Kelly A. Morgan

Personal Reflection:
Finances

Reflect on your finances and answer the questions below based on your level of satisfaction with it.

Describe your current personal financial plan for saving, investing and spending.

_____
_____
_____
_____
_____
_____
_____

What are your fixed, controllable and extra household expenses?

_____
_____
_____
_____
_____
_____

𝒥𝑜𝑢𝑟𝑛𝑒𝑦 to a Place Called THERE

What is working well with how you manage your finances?

_____
_____
_____
_____
_____
_____
_____

In what areas would you like to be more financially savvy to better balance life overall?

_____
_____
_____
_____
_____
_____
_____

Key messages for you from the Balancing Finances section…

_____
_____
_____
_____
_____
_____
_____
_____

Other thoughts that come to mind in regards to your current financial situation:

_____
_____
_____
_____
_____
_____
_____

Personal Reflection:
Notes

Kelly A. Morgan

Journey to a Place Called THERE

REST STOP:
Enjoy the View

Now that you know what THERE is, where you are, and have explored the four compass areas of life, I want you to pause for a moment to put things in perspective. It is imperative for you to understand that getting THERE is important; and *how* you get THERE is equally important. In the coming chapters, you will begin to learn how to get on the road for your journey and ultimately, how to get to your Destination THERE. As you travel, make sure that you take time to "enjoy the view," — the pleasures life has to offer.

How often do we allow ourselves the time and the satisfaction of doing the things that truly bring happiness into our lives?

> Enjoying each day of your life should be
> a basic expectation.

With that said, let me ask you this:

What would happen if you worked 55 hours per week instead of 60 hours?

What if you used the extra five hours to enjoy a date night with your spouse or to take your Godson to his karate class?

What if you used the time to do something nice for yourself?

What a concept!

If your procrastination is the only thing stopping you from seeing your dream become your reality, get out of your way! You deserve to be happy and enjoy life. Make the most out of each day.

Never, ever, ever forget to always keep "enjoying the view" at the forefront of your mind as you proceed on your journey to your place called THERE.

4

Be the Compass Needle

Are you one who lies in bed in the morning with your "to do" list scrolling through your head? Then, at night, do you reflect on how tired you are while also thinking of what you did not accomplish and have to carry over to the next day?

"How can I be so busy during the day and still not do some of the main things I wanted to do?" you ask yourself.

Well, you can always do things differently for one or two days to catch up. But, would it not be better to adjust your patterns to better fit your overall needs on a more consistent basis?

This chapter is probably the most important one of all. We have discussed the four primary areas of life—Relationships, Health, Spirituality and Finances. We have also discussed identifying where you currently are in life and your imbalances. The logical question to ask now is, "How can I pull all of this together so that these concepts will work in real life, in my life?"

Answer: First, there must be awareness, then, there can be change.

A professionally trained and certified leadership or life coach can be your sounding board and accountability partner as you identify your current place in various areas in life, the gaps and barriers between where you want to be and your plan of action for achieving your goals within your desired timeline.

The first point of action is to recognize how to create a healthy, work-life balance for yourself. Too much of anything is not a good thing. Whether your day is filled with the responsibilities of running a household or running a multi-billion dollar enterprise, establishing an appropriate balance and maintaining control is the key to your success.

In the absence of a personal life coach, let's look back at your notes from the *Personal Reflection* pages at the end of each of the previous sections. Which area appears to need the most immediate attention for your life overall? Keep in mind that often times, when you make a change it can create a positive domino effect. Walt Disney said, "We keep moving forward, opening NEW doors and doing NEW things. Our curiosity keeps taking us down NEW paths." Change is not always easy or comfortable. However, when you start to reap the benefits and are enjoying a more fulfilling life, you will thank yourself for enduring the challenges.

Journey **to a Place Called THERE**

Without giving yourself any boundaries, think about how you would want your life to be in the four primary areas. Be specific with your thoughts and write them down below; if you need more space, write them in a personal notebook or journal.

My Visions for My Compass for Life to Get THERE Are:

My vision for my Relationships THERE is…

_____
_____
_____
_____
_____
_____

My vision for my Health THERE is…

_____
_____
_____
_____
_____

My vision for my Spiritual THERE is…

_____

_____

_____

_____

_____

_____

My vision for my Financial THERE is…

_____

_____

_____

_____

_____

_____

Now that you have specified your "dream" situation, let's turn your dreams into your reality! *NOTE: We will do this one at a time, of course, so be sure to focus on the area that is most imbalanced as you continue to read this book; you will of course, go back and repeat to balance the other areas after that! That way, you can be THERE in every key compass area!*

So, have you identified your area? And you are focused on the vision for that area? Great! Let's move on!

To make this ideal situation a reality, ask yourself, "What needs to happen?" Do not focus on why it cannot. Instead, focus on how it can materialize.

For those nagging, negative thoughts of barriers and obstacles, create a separate list entitled "barriers." You will want to think through and identify any barriers that could hinder you from achieving your dream. By foreseeing any obstacles and potential pitfalls to achieving your dreams, one of two things will happen:

1. You will prepare yourself to MOVE THROUGH the barrier without letting it rattle you and move you off of your course. Visualize having an umbrella when threatening storm clouds pour down torrential rain.

2. You will learn to JUMP OVER the barrier and continue on your path. Visualize an Olympic track runner jumping over hurdles in a relay race.

Preparing for the Next Journey

Now that we have identified how you want your life to look, the next question is: When? Keep in mind the barriers you have identified that could get in your way. Then, set a realistic timeline for yourself. This will help you to see exactly how you can turn your dreams into your reality—one step at a time.

Using the scenario from chapter one, let's make this personal and put what you have learned into action. To refresh your memory, here is a summary of the scenario:

You are a married homeowner with three children. With the dual-income, you are able to pay all of the necessary bills each month, but do not have a robust savings account. You have two car notes to pay each month and a small college fund set aside for each of the children. When you go into work today, you are called to an impromptu department meeting where you are informed that a business decision has just re-organized you out of a job—effective immediately. You will receive a severance package of two weeks of pay and medical coverage through the end of the month. What do you do?

Which of the primary life areas of your life will need to be adjusted to regain your life balance?

_____

_____

_____

_____

Given your new situation, what is your goal, your destination THERE?

_____

_____

_____

Journey to a Place Called THERE

What steps do you take as you begin this journey?

___

What barriers do you foresee that you will face on this journey?

___

What milestones will you set for yourself along the way?

___

Since we are making this scenario personal, here is what I would do:

1. Identify the two primary life areas affected initially by losing my job—Health and Finances.

2. If the family is currently on my insurance plan, I would move all of us to my husband's insurance.
   - I would ask my husband to speak with his human resources department to obtain the appropriate forms and information needed to add us onto his insurance plan in the middle of the benefit year.
   - Generally, changes can only be made during open enrollment periods; however, there are exceptions for life events. The benefits information from his company will provide all of the details and deadlines we will need in order to make informed decisions.

3. From the financial perspective, my husband and I would need to create a revised household budget. I would:
   - Review in detail all of our household expenses, income, savings and investments.
   - Use the *Budgeting Worksheet* to identify our fixed, controllable and extra expenses.
   - Determine how much has been spent in the past on the fixed expenses to anticipate upcoming expenses.
   - Identify which controllable expenses could be reduced and which extra expenses could be eliminated.

- Calculate the amount of money we had in our checking, saving, 401(k) and any other investment accounts.
- Allow monies invested in our 401(K) and in other stocks and mutual funds to grow as long as possible for use during retirement.

4. I would update my resume to reflect my most recent job duties and begin my job search.

5. To focus my job search, I would determine if I want to continue in the same industry and career field or if this is a time to make some career changes.
   - My husband and I would discuss what is best for our family regarding my job search and the needs of the household.
   - Together we would determine our overall goal; our destination THERE!

Now, say that we decided that I would pursue a career in business coaching. In that case, I would identify people that could mentor and assist me in my new career. I would create a marketing and business plan to establish a firm business foundation. I would also need to identify the barriers that could prevent me from being a successful business coach and how to avoid these barriers. In addition to identifying the barriers, I would also identify the milestones for my coaching business and our household. This is an important "checks and balances" step to ensure the desire to build my business is not at the expense of the family.

I would also use this time to reflect on all four of the primary life areas, and then, I would ask myself the following:

1. Are there any relationships that I have been neglecting that I can build upon during this time?

2. Are there any family, friends or acquaintances that may be able to help me to build my new business and leadership coaching career?

3. Are there any ministries in the church that could use my talents or community service organizations where I can volunteer?

Since I may not have had the time previously to focus on exercising, paying attention to my diet and mental health, perhaps I would develop a healthier lifestyle for my family and me. Since my husband and I were forced to review and streamline our household budget, there may be some cost-cutting measures that we would continue, which would help us to build up our savings account and the college fund for the kids. Most importantly, I would remain focused on the ultimate goal—my destination THERE!

Inspiration: Do As They Did...

Often times, we do not stretch ourselves to really go after what we want out of life. There are so many naysayers that we encounter along the way and so much self-doubt in our own minds that we defeat ourselves before we give ourselves a chance to succeed.

For instance, when someone begins to play golf, they have to learn to manage mental self-talk, physical strength, technical accuracy and visual assessment. Allow me to introduce you to Wild Bill!

Wild Bill truly earned that nickname. Whenever Wild Bill would hit a golf ball it might veer to the left, to the right or even behind him. Those persons playing in the foursomes with him soon learned that the sport of golf was more dangerous than expected. To learn to control the golf ball and perfect his swing, Wild Bill watched videos, studied the golf magazines he subscribed to each month, created his own "golf course" in the basement of his home and practiced his golf swing with an old golf club. Of course, eventually, Wild Bill learned how to make the golf ball soar through the air appropriately, going around the dog legs, over the sand traps and water, landing almost effortlessly on the green! Wild Bill, my dad, lived each day to the fullest, loved life, being with his family and playing the game of golf. When on the golf course with friends and family, he was in his "place called THERE!"

A simple path probably seems safer and easier to reach. My mom used to tell me to "Shoot for the moon and you're sure to land amongst the stars." So I say to you, aim high with your dreams. You just might surprise yourself and encourage others to do the same.

Oprah Winfrey is a wonderful example of someone who has successfully set goals and realized, if not exceeded, her own dreams. Ms. Winfrey has shattered the glass ceiling financially for women. With her talk show and magazine, she has also redefined the communication and media professions. And, she is inspiring people by the millions with her motto…Live your best life! Yes, I admire Ms. Winfrey because of her accomplishments, but even more so because she has not forgotten from where she has come. Regardless of her fame, she gives back to the community and understands the impact she has globally.

Though people worldwide are aware of Ms. Winfrey's successes, certainly she had some failures along the way…and may even still experience some today. That is important for you to understand because it is inevitable that not all ideas and attempts will be successful. Not all dreams will be realized. The wonderful thing is…it is okay! It is actually expected that we will make mistakes. Just do not let a mistake or failure hinder you from continuing to pursue your dreams. Mistakes and failures provide a second, third and sometimes, a fourth chance to turn a situation around and start down a new path in life.

So, seize the new opportunities and continue to dream! Because without a dream, there is no vision, without a vision, there is no goal and no way to chart your course to your place called THERE. Dreams are important and do not let anyone tell you different…EVER!

Admittedly, some daydreams are just fantasies that will never come true. Some daydreams are foreshadows of your future that simply require more focus for them to become your new reality. Do not try to sort out which is which, just dream. The combination of positive self-thought and a strategic plan of action can lead to success. As you dream, remember this:

"But in the unlikely story that is America, there has never been anything false about hope. For when we have faced down impossible odds, when we've been told that we're not ready, or that we shouldn't try, or that we can't, generations of Americans have responded with a simple creed that sums up the spirit of a people. Yes we can!"

~ President Barack Obama

...and Coach Kelly echoes, "Yes you can!"

Kelly A. Morgan

Personal Reflection:
Notes

www.CoachKellySpeaks.com *or* www.SAGE-PS.com

Journey to a Place Called THERE

5

Destination: THERE

By this time, you have looked at your life honestly. So, you know where your needs are in your life. You have searched your mind and your heart and know what dreams you have for your life. Each goal, each ultimate dream is your destination THERE. Some of you have multiple THEREs you would like to reach, but some of you may have just one; either way is fine. Everyone's situation is different. If you do have goals in multiple areas, realize that you do not have to work on them simultaneously. Remember: This is about you, so work at your own pace. The important thing is that you get THERE. With that said, let's head out on the Journey to *Your* Place Called THERE...

Consider this scenario: You look at your life and are pleased with the current condition of your relationships, health and spirituality. Recognizing that, of course, there is always room for improvement, but the obvious need in your life is around your finances. You have five goals in the area of finances that you would love to reach but, for whatever reasons, you have not been successful in the past. Today, you make the commitment to yourself to begin your journey towards five financial destinations. Financially, you will be in your "Place Called THERE" when you are able to:

1. Carry a zero balance on your credit cards

2. Build up your retirement savings account to a $500,000 balance

3. Develop the self-discipline to maintain the monthly household budget you have created using the *Budgeting Worksheet*

4. Organize your finances well enough so that you can teach your children how to properly manage their finances in the future

5. Put aside $5,000 each year to take a family vacation and spend more time with friends

With each of these goals, there are milestones to be reached along the journey. As with any journey, there will be obstacles in the way. But once you see the credit card balances fading away, imagine the joy, feeling of accomplishment, and how motivated you will be to continue on this financial journey to your ultimate Destination THERE.

Now, imagine the excitement and pride you will feel when you have arrived at your Destination THERE! When you are able to pay off your credit cards in full each month and

Journey to a Place Called THERE

carry a zero balance. You have reached your Destination THERE! The even more wonderful fact is you can feel the same joy as you exhibit the self-discipline to stick to your household budget each month, which assisted you in reaching this initial destination. Look! You have just arrived at your next Destination THERE!

By no longer having the large finance charges assessed to your credit cards, you can use that money for your annual family vacation and to go towards your retirement savings account. Destination THERE! Destination THERE!!

Now that you have elevated your finances to being more organized, you are in a better place to begin teaching your children how they can become more financially savvy. Can you guess where that takes you? You guessed it— Destination THERE!

By having your finances more in order, your health will probably be improved since you will no longer have this financial stress in your life. Your relationships may be improved since you are able to spend more time together with family and friends. If you are led to give tithes and offerings at church or make donations to non-profit organizations, your spiritual life will be improved as well.

Wow! You made the commitment to yourself to change one primary area of your life and it affected the other areas as well! It is a wonderful feeling to set a goal for yourself, overcome the obstacles along the way, enjoy your accomplishment and then to celebrate YOU!

Kelly A. Morgan

Setting Out on Your Destination THERE

So, now that you have read the chapters and completed the *Personal Reflection Questions* for each of the primary life areas—Relationships, Health, Spirituality and Finances—what's next?

Before we move forward, take a few minutes to look back at your notes and responses to each of the *Personal Reflection Questions*. If you were honest with yourself and took the time to reflect on the meaning of each question as it directly relates to you, you should be able to identify which areas are working well and which areas could use some improvement. If you have additional thoughts that you want to include for any of the *Personal Reflection Questions*, feel free to do so at this time.

The *Personal Reflection Questions* were specifically developed to stimulate your mind for thinking on a deeper level. It is important for you to identify the areas of life that are not going well, acknowledge the areas in which you are satisfied with the current conditions and visualize the ideal Destination THERE for each of the primary life areas.

In the next chapter, *Destination THERE Roadmaps*, you will have an opportunity to expand on your thoughts and answers from the *Reflection Questions* in previous chapters. By working through the *Destination THERE Roadmaps*, you will begin to create an action plan for yourself to guide you towards your desired destination!

Tips for Getting THERE

- Dream big! Think of the ideal situation, and then in your mind, move your thoughts backwards from the ideal to current day. Specifically, consider what will need to happen to transform your ideal situation into your current day reality.

- Develop your plan to manage obstacles (they're inevitable!) so that they will not hinder you from continuing on your journey. What obstacles or barriers may get in your path along the way? Make a list and be ready to conquer them!

- Divide each goal into sensible milestones that build upon each other until you ultimately achieve the goal.

- Establish a timeline for completing the milestone and for reaching your ultimate Destination THERE. This is crucial! The milestones allow you to see how far you have come on your journey and will help make reaching your Destination THERE more manageable.

- Plan for roadblocks and be flexible. When unforeseen circumstances happen and if you are unable to meet your initial timeline, know that you have not failed; the failure would be allowing the new obstacle to discourage you and dissolve your plans completely. Instead, forge ahead on your journey by simply adjusting your timeline and continuing to move forward.

- Celebrate! Accomplishing a goal also takes commitment and dedication from you so it is important to celebrate the milestones on the road to achieving your major dreams. Celebrations for accomplishing your goals can be as simple or elaborate as you like. You may decide to treat yourself to an ice cream cone, buy yourself something nice, or have a fun night out with friends. You decide how to celebrate!

By setting a realistic timeline, identifying obstacles, planning how you will manage barriers and establishing milestones, your dreams can become your reality!

Inspiration for Your Journey to *Your* Place Called THERE

For a tree to grow strong and be long-lived, it must grow lots of deep roots first and then slowly puts on the top growth of branches, leaves and flowers. By growing a stable foundation first, the tree will be more resistant to the stress and strain of the environment in which it is planted. The tree symbolizes how we should build our lives and relationships. We should focus on building a strong foundation for our lives before branching off into new areas. Take time for honest reflection of your life. What legacy do you hope to leave on the world?

Journey to a Place Called THERE

Be true to yourself in all you say and do. Expect and work towards excellence in all areas of life. Most importantly, remember to keep a balance between relationships, health, spirituality and finances as you pursue your dreams and travel to your next destination...on your journey to a place called THERE.

So, are you ready? Then hit the road...

Kelly A. Morgan

Personal Reflection:
Notes

_____
_____
_____
_____
_____
_____
_____
_____
_____
_____
_____
_____
_____
_____
_____

Journey to a Place Called THERE

Journey to a Place Called THERE

6

My Destination THERE
Roadmaps

Like a diary or daily journal, *Journey to a Place Called THERE* is your personal navigation guide. It holds your thoughts, likes, dislikes and promises to yourself to make the changes in your life that are necessary to move you towards the life you deserve and desire. Now that you have had the opportunity to make notes on the *Personal Reflections* pages as well as to answer the *Personal Reflection Questions*, it's time to take action!

In the following pages of this chapter, you will find two *My Destination THERE Roadmaps* for each of the primary life areas: Balancing Relationships, Balancing Health, Balancing Spirituality and Balancing Finances. There are also two additional blank *My Destination THERE Roadmaps* to use for the primary life area of your choice. Since you may have more than one goal in either of the primary life areas, the additional *My Destination THERE Roadmaps* are included. This is your personal guide book, your personal journal. You may not have any goals for certain primary life areas today, but next month,

- *95* -

next year, you may, so the *My Destination THERE Roadmaps* will be available for you.

To complete the *My Destination THERE Roadmaps*, you may utilize either your notes from the previous *Personal Reflection* pages or where your heart is telling you that you need to focus your attention. Identify your ultimate goal for that particular primary life area and when it should be completed. Your ultimate goal is your Destination THERE. Depending on the complexity of the goal, you can then identify the milestones to reach along the journey and any potential barriers. In identifying the barriers, you will also want to plan on how you will move through or move around them, should the barriers arise. As with any journey in life, there are always lessons to learn that will prepare you for the next journey. Make a few notes for yourself as key points to remember.

After being on this journey, at some point you will ask yourself, "Are we there yet?" So, how will you know when you have reached your destination? Identify the characteristics of achieving your goal and finally arriving at your Destination THERE! One wonderful aspect of setting goals, determining key milestones along the way and identifying barriers is that you will be able to see in a more concrete manner the details of what you overcame during your journey to arrive at your destination.

Now, for the equally important and most fun piece… celebrating your accomplishment! Be proud and celebrate you! You have just taken another step towards creating and maintaining the balanced life you desire and deserve!

Journey to a Place Called THERE

Kelly A. Morgan

My Destination THERE
Roadmap:
Balancing Relationships

My goal / Destination THERE is:

_____
_____
_____
_____
_____
_____

Milestones to reach my Destination THERE are:

milestone *mm/dd/yy*

_____
_____
_____

www.CoachKellySpeaks.com *or* **www.SAGE-PS.com**

Journey to a Place Called THERE

My completion / arrival date is:

_____
_____
_____
_____

I anticipate the following barriers:

_____
_____
_____
_____

I will move around or move through barriers by:

_____
_____
_____
_____

Lessons learned along this journey include:

_____
_____
_____
_____

I will celebrate arriving at my Destination THERE by:

_____
_____

Kelly A. Morgan

My Destination THERE
Roadmap:
Balancing Relationships

My goal / Destination THERE is:

_____
_____
_____
_____
_____
_____
_____

Milestones to reach my Destination THERE are:

milestone   *mm/dd/yy*

_____
_____
_____

www.CoachKellySpeaks.com *or* **www.SAGE-PS.com**

Journey to a Place Called THERE

My completion / arrival date is:

_____
_____
_____
_____

I anticipate the following barriers:

_____
_____
_____
_____

I will move around or move through barriers by:

_____
_____
_____
_____

Lessons learned along this journey include:

_____
_____
_____
_____

I will celebrate arriving at my Destination THERE by:

_____
_____

Kelly A. Morgan

My Destination THERE
Roadmap:
Balancing Health

My goal / Destination THERE is:

_____
_____
_____
_____
_____
_____
_____

Milestones to reach my Destination THERE are:

milestone   *mm/dd/yy*

_____
_____
_____

www.CoachKellySpeaks.com *or* **www.SAGE-PS.com**

Journey to a Place Called THERE

My completion / arrival date is:

_____

_____

_____

_____

I anticipate the following barriers:

_____

_____

_____

_____

I will move around or move through barriers by:

_____

_____

_____

_____

Lessons learned along this journey include:

_____

_____

_____

_____

I will celebrate arriving at my Destination THERE by:

_____

_____

Kelly A. Morgan

My Destination THERE
Roadmap:
Balancing Health

My goal / Destination THERE is:

_____
_____
_____
_____
_____
_____

Milestones to reach my Destination THERE are:

milestone   *mm/dd/yy*

_____
_____
_____

www.CoachKellySpeaks.com *or* **www.SAGE-PS.com**

Journey to a Place Called THERE

My completion / arrival date is:

_____

_____

_____

_____

I anticipate the following barriers:

_____

_____

_____

_____

I will move around or move through barriers by:

_____

_____

_____

_____

Lessons learned along this journey include:

_____

_____

_____

_____

I will celebrate arriving at my Destination THERE by:

_____

_____

Kelly A. Morgan

My Destination THERE
Roadmap:
Balancing Spirituality

My goal / Destination THERE is:

_____
_____
_____
_____
_____
_____
_____

Milestones to reach my Destination THERE are:

milestone   *mm/dd/yy*

_____
_____
_____

www.CoachKellySpeaks.com *or* **www.SAGE-PS.com**

Journey to a Place Called THERE

My completion / arrival date is:

_____

_____

_____

_____

I anticipate the following barriers:

_____

_____

_____

_____

I will move around or move through barriers by:

_____

_____

_____

_____

Lessons learned along this journey include:

_____

_____

_____

_____

I will celebrate arriving at my Destination THERE by:

_____

_____

Kelly A. Morgan

My Destination THERE
Roadmap:
Balancing Spirituality

My goal / Destination THERE is:

_____
_____
_____
_____
_____
_____
_____

Milestones to reach my Destination THERE are:

milestone   *mm/dd/yy*

_____
_____
_____

www.CoachKellySpeaks.com *or* **www.SAGE-PS.com**

Journey to a Place Called THERE

My completion / arrival date is:

_____
_____
_____
_____

I anticipate the following barriers:

_____
_____
_____
_____

I will move around or move through barriers by:

_____
_____
_____
_____

Lessons learned along this journey include:

_____
_____
_____
_____

I will celebrate arriving at my Destination THERE by:

_____
_____

Kelly A. Morgan

My Destination THERE
Roadmap:
Balancing Finances

My goal / Destination THERE is:

_____
_____
_____
_____
_____
_____
_____

Milestones to reach my Destination THERE are:

milestone   *mm/dd/yy*

_____
_____
_____

www.CoachKellySpeaks.com *or* **www.SAGE-PS.com**

Journey to a Place Called THERE

My completion / arrival date is:

_____

_____

_____

_____

I anticipate the following barriers:

_____

_____

_____

_____

I will move around or move through barriers by:

_____

_____

_____

_____

Lessons learned along this journey include:

_____

_____

_____

_____

I will celebrate arriving at my Destination THERE by:

_____

_____

Kelly A. Morgan

My Destination THERE
Roadmap:
Balancing Finances

My goal / Destination THERE is:

_____
_____
_____
_____
_____
_____

Milestones to reach my Destination THERE are:

milestone   *mm/dd/yy*

_____
_____
_____

www.CoachKellySpeaks.com *or* **www.SAGE-PS.com**

Journey to a Place Called THERE

My completion / arrival date is:

___

I anticipate the following barriers:

___

I will move around or move through barriers by:

___

Lessons learned along this journey include:

___

I will celebrate arriving at my Destination THERE by:

___

Kelly A. Morgan

My Destination THERE
Roadmap:
Balancing _____

My goal / Destination THERE is:

_____
_____
_____
_____
_____
_____
_____

Milestones to reach my Destination THERE are:

milestone   *mm/dd/yy*

_____
_____
_____

www.CoachKellySpeaks.com *or* **www.SAGE-PS.com**

Journey to a Place Called THERE

My completion / arrival date is:

_____
_____
_____
_____

I anticipate the following barriers:

_____
_____
_____
_____

I will move around or move through barriers by:

_____
_____
_____
_____

Lessons learned along this journey include:

_____
_____
_____
_____

I will celebrate arriving at my Destination THERE by:

_____
_____

Kelly A. Morgan

My Destination THERE
Roadmap:
Balancing _____

My goal / Destination THERE is:

_____
_____
_____
_____
_____
_____
_____

Milestones to reach my Destination THERE are:

milestone   *mm/dd/yy*

_____
_____
_____

www.CoachKellySpeaks.com *or* **www.SAGE-PS.com**

Journey to a Place Called THERE

My completion / arrival date is:

_____

_____

_____

_____

I anticipate the following barriers:

_____

_____

_____

_____

I will move around or move through barriers by:

_____

_____

_____

_____

Lessons learned along this journey include:

_____

_____

_____

_____

I will celebrate arriving at my Destination THERE by:

_____

_____

Journey to a Place Called THERE

Coach Kelly Speaks

You might be wondering what happened with the ultimatum I was given—to maintain my coaching business or my employment. Although it seemed closing my coaching business was the simple decision to make so that I could keep my job, every bone in my body told me it was the wrong decision for me. The only thing I knew for sure is that I could not go back to an unhealthy work environment that stressed me out to the point of migraine headaches every day. At that point, my health and sanity meant more to me than anything.

There were many days when I sat quietly at home and thought about what really made me happy in my professional career. What was it that pulled me into the field of Human Resources so many years ago? I remembered that I wanted to see people working in careers they enjoyed. It was rewarding to help prepare people to live the life they desired.

Friends and I prayed that my situation would be given to God and that His grace, mercy and favor would shine on me. After months of soul searching, frustrating tearful nights, prayer, heart-to-heart talks with my mom and close friends, I finally paid attention to the burning desire in my soul. I had a strong feeling come over me that something wonderful was going to happen with my business. This was a feeling of both peace of mind and encouragement.

So, I reprioritized my life and made a decision: I resigned. It was a frightening and exciting decision that forced me to chart a course for my new THERE, but I took solace in knowing that I would not be alone on my journey.

That feeling, coupled with the support of my friends and family, the rebalancing of my own life, and identifying my new destination THERE led me to where I am today. The fact that you have this book in your hands is a dream that has become my reality. I am in my "place called THERE!"

For years, I dreamt of writing a book and owning a successful business. Obstacles, excuses and life kept getting in my way. Finally, during a period of rest, I put pen to paper and started writing. I decided to follow my goals and my dreams and step out on faith. I started writing down my thoughts and several book ideas came to me. I started writing a revised business plan to incorporate my new-found direction for my life and my business. I hired Scribe, Etc. (www.scribe-etc.com) to manage the full book self-publishing process from copy editing to book layout to pre and post-publishing marketing. Scribe, Etc.

also developed my branding and marketing material for the expansion of my coaching business, entitled *Coach Kelly Speaks*, which highlights the inspirational speaker and author aspects of my business.

My vision for *Coach Kelly Speaks* is to be an accountability coach, strategic business partner and inspirational voice to encourage individuals to achieve their goals and exceed even their wildest expectations for themselves. The main focus areas of *Coach Kelly Speaks* include:

- Preparing individuals for success in the world of work
- Building a stronger foundation for the future generations
- Mentoring young adults
- Creating a balanced life overall

I am happy to say that with the publication of this, my first book, I am THERE! It is truly a wonderful feeling and a positive culmination of a difficult period in my life. Since I have accomplished my dream of writing a book and am now a true entrepreneur, I celebrated my success! I went to one of my favorite stores at the mall, Coach, and I bought myself a bottle of the new Coach perfume. I thought that was a very appropriate way to celebrate! After all, I am *Coach* Kelly!

By making the decision to continue coaching and expanding my business with *Coach Kelly Speaks*, my world feels aligned and balanced. I am happy now! I have the ability to flex my schedule to allow for much more time with friends and family, to work in ministries in my church, to continue our mission of "service to all mankind" with my sophisticated sorority sisters of Alpha Kappa Alpha Sorority, Incorporated, while also maintaining my health and a better overall quality of life.

The Journey Continues...

I am proud of what I have accomplished thus far, reaching one of my THEREs. However, I know that in actuality my work is not done. This accomplishment is actually a milestone for the larger dreams, more grand THEREs that I have for myself. Still, it is my pleasure to share my story, my journey, with you. I also feel it is my duty for three main reasons…

1. To let you know that you do have a say in how you live your life

2. To inspire you to take the first step towards your goals, whatever they may be

3. To help you realize that you do not have to believe everything people say about you; forecast your own future

Taking the first few steps towards your goals may be frightening since it is new territory. But, it can also be exciting and so very rewarding! So, how about it? I did it, and so can you! Whatever you see for you in your future…go for it! Start making plans and taking action towards your future, today! Know that there will be barriers and obstacles in your path. Create your plan for how you will maneuver through or around these obstacles. Then keep moving on the path of your dream, for your future, to your place called THERE!

Never settle for good when your good could be better, and your better could be your best yet!

- Kelly

I almost forgot...

It may not seem like it yet, but this is a reciprocal relationship. I hope that I've inspired you by sharing my story and the lessons I learned. However, I am not finished. My life, and thus my journey, is a work in progress and though I hope that this book inspires you to be what you aspire to be, know that your journey story will inspire others, and feed my soul. So, please **SHARE YOUR STORY WITH ME!**

Let me know how you're doing along your journey to your place called THERE. Send me an email with a note and a picture, a video or an audio message with your updates. I'd love to hear from you and will share your stories with others to inspire them too!

> **Email your journey story to: Info@CoachKellySpeaks.com!**

Journey **to a Place Called THERE**

Other Points of Interest

The next section consists of various quotes, scriptures, short stories and poems that speak to me and helped me through my journey while also complimenting the four primary areas of life: Relationships, Health, Spirituality and Finances. Since this book is a navigation guide, I wanted to include a few additional tools that you may choose to use if you so desire. If you like poetry, I encourage you to write or find a poem that speaks to your heart and helps you succeed as you travel along your journey. If you are more spiritual and find the assistance you desire in biblical scriptures, I invite you to identify a few scriptures that help to keep you grounded in faith and motivated to continue your journey. Whatever sayings, quotes, short stories, etc. that you find, I encourage you to write them down in this guide book so you can refer back to them while you travel along your journey.

Other Points of Interest

"Serenity Prayer"

God grant me
the Serenity to accept the things I
cannot change; the Courage to change
the things I can, and wisdom to know
the difference;

Living one day at a time; Accepting
hardship as a pathway to peace; Taking,
as Jesus did, this sinful world as it is,
not as I would have it:

Trusting that you will make all things
right if I surrender to your will; that I may
be reasonably happy in this life and supremely
happy with you forever in the next.

~ *Boethius, philosopher (circa 500 A.D.)*

"Footprints in the Sand"

One night I dreamed I was walking along the beach with the Lord. Many scenes from my life flashed across the sky. In each scene I noticed footprints in the sand. Sometimes there were two sets of footprints, other times there was one only.

This bothered me because I noticed that during the low periods of my life, when I was suffering from anguish, sorrow or defeat, I could see only one set of footprints, so I said to the Lord, "You promised me Lord, that if I followed you, you would walk with me always. But I have noticed that during the most trying periods of my life there has only been one set of footprints in the sand. Why, when I needed you most, have you not been there for me?"

The Lord replied,
"The years when you have seen only one set of footprints, my child, is when I carried you."

~ *Mary Stevenson*

Other Points of Interest

Success is loving life and daring to live it.

~ *Maya Angelou*

Let us not become weary in doing good, for at the proper time we will reap a harvest if we do not give up.

~ *Galatians 6:9 NIV*

The road we have taken to this point has not been easy. But, then again, the road to change never is.

~ *President Barack Obama*

Q
U
O
T
E
S

Let us throw off everything that hinders and the sin that so easily entangles, and let us run with perseverance the race marked out for us.

~ Hebrews 12:1 NIV

A bend in the road is not the end of the road... unless you fail to make the turn.

~ Author Unknown

We also glory in tribulation, knowing that tribulation produces perseverance; and perseverance, character; and character, hope.

~ Romans 5:3-4

Other Points of Interest

A few years ago, a friend gave me a prayer that her pastor wrote. This prayer is purposely kept visibly on my refrigerator. Below are some excerpts from this prayer that I recited several times each week (and still do!) that touched my spirit.

"Declaration of Favor"

Father, in the name of Jesus, I thank you that the set time for favor on my life is now. I choose to walk in favor of God, in every area of my life. I am the righteousness of God because of what Jesus did for me on Calvary. Therefore, favor surrounds me as a shield. Father, I thank you, because of supernatural favor on my life, and on my family's life, we're delivered out of all conflict and dispute. Father I thank you that favor brings prominence, allowing me to be brought into places that others will marvel over. I release my faith now, for genuine friendships, that I will be a Godly example, in other's lives. Thank you Father, that favor, causes petition to be granted, from hostile authorities.

I understand, it's through my praise, that I accelerate the favor of God. So Father, I honor you, I worship you, I adore you, I praise you, for you alone, can cause others, to go out of their way, to use their power, their ability, and their influence, to help me. And as your child, I come boldly now, before the throne of grace. I find mercy, for my own failures, but I also find favor, just when I need it. So Father, I thank you, for supernatural favor in my life, now, in Jesus' name, Amen!!!

Other Points of Interest

Live well. Laugh often. Love much.

~ *Lori Siebert*

Love is patient, love is kind.
It does not envy, it does not boast,
it is not proud.
It is not rude, it is not self-seeking,
it is not easily angered, it keeps
no record of wrongs.
Love does not delight in evil but rejoices
with the truth. It always protects, always
trusts, always hopes, always perseveres.
Love never fails.

~ *1 Corinthians 13:4-7*

If you're not riding the wave of change,
you'll find yourself beneath it.

~ *Author Unknown*

Friends are flowers in the garden of life!

~ Lori Siebert

The big secret in life is there is no secret.
Whatever your goal, you can get there if
you're willing to work.

~ Oprah Winfrey

When patterns are broken,
new worlds emerge.

~ Tuli Kupferburg

Kelly A. Morgan

Other Points of Interest

The following is a piece that a family member gave to me. In fact, she framed it for me. It's been displayed in my home ever since. Perhaps it'll find its way to a coffee table in your home.

"Untitled / The Philospher's Stones"

A philosophy professor stood before his class and had some items in front of him. When class began, wordlessly, he picked up a large empty mayonnaise jar and proceeded to fill it up with rocks about 2" in diameter. He then asked the students if the jar was full. They agreed that it was. So then the professor picked up a box of pebbles and poured them into the jar. He shook the jar. The pebbles, of course, rolled into the open areas between he rocks. The students laughed. He then added a box of sand. Of course the sand filled everything else.

(con't.)

www.CoachKellySpeaks.com *or* www.SAGE-PS.com

QUOTES

"Now," said the professor. "I want you to recognize this as your life. The ROCKS are the important things—your FAMILY, your PARTNER, your HEALTH—anything that is so important that if it were lost…you would be nearly destroyed. The pebbles are the other things that matter to you like your job, your house, and your car. The sand is everything else. The small stuff. If you put the sand in the jar first, there is no room for the pebbles and the rocks. If you spend your energy and time on the small stuff, you will never have room for the things that are important to you. Pay attention to the things that are important to your happiness. Play with your children. Take time to get medical check-ups. Go dancing with your mate. There will always be time to go to work, clean the house, give a dinner party, go to meetings and fix stuff around the house.

Take care of the rocks first—the things that really matter. Set your priorities. The rest is just sand.

~ Author Unknown

Other Points of Interest

Judge your success by
what you had to give up to get it.

~ *Dalai Lama*

Changes in life are inevitable and
not always controllable. What can be
controlled is how to manage, react to and
work through the change process.

~ *Kelly A Morgan*

Live a good, honorable life.
Then, when you get older and think back,
you'll be able to enjoy it a second time.

~ *Dalai Lama*

About the Author

Kelly A. Morgan is a real-world and real-talk inspirational speaker, author and business coach. As an inspirational speaker and author, Kelly does not simply motivate people to do just anything; instead, she inspires individuals to do what they aspire to do but have not had the encouragement and support to do in the past. Her first book, *Journey to a Place Called THERE: A Navigation Guide for Creating a Balanced Life*, is a prime example of that. The book focuses on the importance of having four key areas of life aligned and includes worksheets to help readers plot a course for realizing their dreams.

In addition to being an inspirational author and speaker, Kelly is also the Owner and CEO of SAGE Professional Strategies LLC, a business and leadership coaching firm. As a Business and Leadership Coach, Kelly uses her corporate Human Resource experience and professional certified coach training to be the catalyst for entrepreneurs, executives, small businesses and religious organizations to create and implement their personal and professional development plans. Her credentials include:

- Bachelor and Master Degrees in Human Resources
- International Coach Federation Associate Certified Coach
- Certified Legacy Leadership® Facilitator
- Trained in Lean Sigma and Lean Event Facilitation

When she is not speaking, coaching, or working on a book project, Kelly keeps busy by staying involved in various organizations. She is a member of the International Speakers Network, Society for Human Resource Management, Alpha Kappa Alpha Sorority, Incorporated, Cincinnati USA Regional Chamber and National Black MBA Association.

For more information on the professional services Kelly offers, or to request "Coach Kelly" as a speaker for your next event, visit

CoachKelly speaks

www.CoachKellySpeaks.com!

Journey
to a Place Called
THERE

A Navigation Guide for Creating a Balanced Life

www.ingramcontent.com/pod-product-compliance
Lightning Source LLC
Chambersburg PA
CBHW071725090426
42738CB00009B/1875